Book One
God

A First Look
The Christian Faith

LION
Children's Books

Bible passages mentioned in this book:

1   Psalm 24, verses 1 and 2.
2   Psalm 104, verses 10 to 12, and 18.
3   Psalm 65, verses 9 to 11.
4   Psalm 100.
5   Genesis, chapters 7 to 9; also Psalm 7, verses 10 and 11.
6   Psalm 119, especially verses 4 and 105.
7   Luke, chapter 15, verses 11 to 32.
8   Psalm 131.
9   Matthew, chapter 12, verse 50.
10 Psalm 23.
11 Psalm 68, verses 7 to 10, and 20.
12 Psalm 25, verses 11 to 14.
13 2 Corinthians, chapter 3, verse 18; also 2 Timothy, chapter 1, verse 7.

Text by Lois Rock
Educational consultant: Margaret Dean
Illustrations copyright © 1994 Carolyn Cox
This edition copyright © 2003 Lion Publishing

The moral rights of the author and illustrator
have been asserted

Published by
Lion Publishing plc
Mayfield House, 256 Banbury Road,
Oxford OX2 7DH, England
www.lion-publishing.co.uk
ISBN 0 7459 4780 8

First published as separate volumes
God, The Bible, Jesus, The Church in 1994
This one volume edition 2003
10 9 8 7 6 5 4 3 2 1 0

Contents

Who is God?   Introduction

The sky   1

Living things   2

Our food   3

Good times   4

Bad times   5

Rules   6

Dads   7

Mums   8

Families   9

People who care   10

Being rescued   11

Friends   12

Air   13

Introduction
Who is
God?

Who is God?
And why do people talk about him?
You can't see anyone called God!
So what *can* people know about him?
Does he exist at all?

Christians believe there is a God.
They read about him in their special book,
the Bible, which includes writings that Jews
read and stories that Muslims know.

In the Bible, Christians read about the things God has done, the things he has said.
They discover more about the God—

● who made the world, and looks after it

who loves good and hates evil

● who cares for people, and wants them to be his friends

who is more powerful than anything in the world, even though no one can see him.

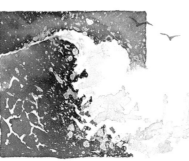

In this book, you can discover some of the things the Bible says about God.

1 Let's look at
The sky

Have you seen the sky?
The golden sun high above
you...
the shimmering blueness
reaching down to the far
horizon...
drifting clouds, silver, white
and grey...
the sliver of a crescent
moon slicing through the
blackness of night...
the glittering stars...
the whole universe.
Have you ever wondered
how it came to be the way
it is?
Or why it exists at all?

Throughout the ages, many people have believed that the world exists because God made it.
That is what Christians today believe.
This is a song from the Bible, written hundreds of years ago, by people who believed in God.

The whole world
and everything in it
belongs to God
who made it.

From Psalm 24 of the Bible

God is the maker of the world.

2 Let's look at

Living things

Think of all the plants and animals
in the world ...
in mountains
deserts,
meadows,
forests,
seas,
cities ...
everywhere!

Thousands of years ago, the people who
lived in a country called Israel looked with
amazement at the wonderful world around
them. They believed that God had made it all.

Today, Christians still sing the song the
Israelites sang to him long ago:

You make springs flow in the valleys,
and rivers run between the hills.
They provide water for the wild animals;
there the wild donkeys drink the water they need.
In the trees nearby
the birds make their nests and sing.
The wild goats live in the high mountains,
and rock hyraxes hide in the cliffs.

From Psalm 104 of the Bible

God is the giver of life.

3 Let's look at
Our food

The sun shines,
the rain falls,
to make plants grow.
There is so much to harvest...
leaves,
stems,
roots,
fruits,
seeds...
food for
people
and animals.

Long ago, the farmers in Israel thanked God for making a world that produced good harvests.

Christians use the same song to thank God for the way he cares for them and all the world.

You provide the earth with crops ... you send rain on the ploughed fields and soak them with water; you soften the soil with showers and make young plants grow. What a rich harvest your goodness provides!
From Psalm 65 of the Bible

God provides everything people need.

4 Let's look at
Good times

Isn't it great
when everything works
out right.
When people are loving,
fair and kind.
When the world seems
full of new life,
new hope,
new joy.
When everything seems
just right,
as it should be.

The Bible says
that when God made the world
it was very good.

Here is a joyful song from
the Bible
that Christians sing to God.

Come on everyone,
sing to God,
come to him,
with your joyful songs.
He made us,
we belong to him,
he takes care of us...
God is good:
his love never changes
and it will last for ever.
From Psalm 100 of the Bible

God is good.

5 Let's look at
Bad times

We don't like to think about bad times:
about people who are unkind,
who quarrel and fight.
About how people get hurt.
About how things get broken.
About the bad things
that make the whole world
a sad place.

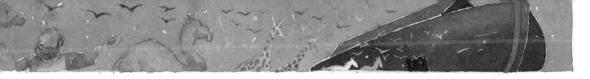

Christians believe that God made a good world and that he hates it when people choose to do bad things. Their wrongdoing has spoiled it all.
It has become a cruel place: there is hurting and death, and great unhappiness.

Once, God sent a flood to destroy all the evil in the world. Even so, he saved Noah, because he was a good man, along with his family and two of every kind of creature.

God takes care of those who live as he wants
but is angry with those who do wrong;
he is a good and fair judge.

From Psalm 7 of the Bible

God is always fair.

6 Let's look at
Rules

Imagine being in a forest
where there were no paths...
Trying to find your way
would be hard in daytime
but even harder at night.
But imagine that you find a path
that leads you
where you want to go.
Would you even think of going off the
path?

Rules can be like a path
that shows you where to go,
that keeps you out of trouble.
The Bible says
that when people disobeyed God
they lost their way
and didn't know how they should live.
God gave them rules,
laws,
to guide them.

Dear God,
you have given us your laws
and told us to obey them
all through our lives...
They show us the path we should
follow.
The people who stay on that path
will find real happiness...
and you will keep them safe.

From Psalm 119 of the Bible

God has given laws to guide people.

7 Let's look at
Dads

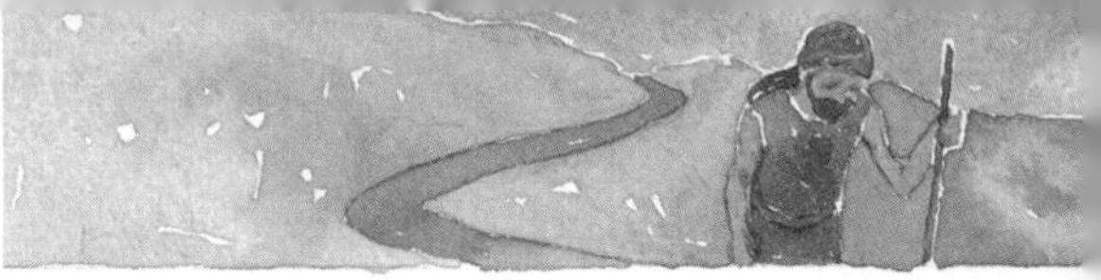

There are all kinds of
dads:
best of all is a dad
who really loves you,
who knows what is
best for you.

Jesus Christ, the person who Christians are named after, told a story about a really loving father.

There was once a young man who didn't want to live at home any more. He took his share of the family money and went off to have a good time.

He spent all his money. Then he couldn't get a job. He didn't have any food. He thought: The people who work on Dad's farm live better than this. Why don't I go home?

He travelled back. How stupid he'd been. What a waste of the family money. What would he say? What excuse did he have?

But his dad saw him coming while he was still a long way off. He went rushing out to meet him.

He welcomed him home, and threw a party!

And that, said Jesus, is how God welcomes anyone who stops doing bad things, who decides to come back to God and live as he wants.

From the book Luke wrote about Jesus in the Bible

God is a loving father.

8 Let's look at

Mums

Mums can be many things:
it's great to have a mum who
really loves you whatever you
do, who knows what to do
when you're scared,
who looks after you when
you're ill.

Long ago, a grown-up wrote this prayer:

Dear God,
I have stopped worrying
about all the things
I cannot control.
Instead, I trust in you
to take care of me,
and I feel as safe
as a child
in its mother's arms.

From Psalm 131 of the Bible

God is like a loving mother.

9 Let's look at
Families

Think about families:
parents, brothers and sisters.
It can be good to have
them around
because they understand
what it's like
to live in your home.
They know what kind of
problems you face.
They might even help you
out.

Christians believe that
God himself
came to this world
as the baby Jesus
and grew up
in an ordinary family.
He knows what it's like
to live in this world
and how hard it can be
to do what is right.
Jesus said this:

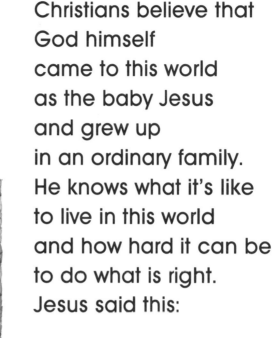

Whoever does what
God wants
is my brother, my sister
and my mother.

**From the book Matthew wrote
about Jesus in the Bible**

**God is like someone in
your family who really
understands and cares.**

10 Let's look at
People who care

It's hard work looking after things.

Imagine looking after a flock of sheep.

Long ago, in Israel, a young boy called David had to look after his flock of sheep.
He had to find them food and water,
he had to protect them from danger.
When he was older he became a soldier and faced even worse dangers.
But he believed that just as he had looked after his sheep,
God was looking after him.

This is a song that David wrote :

God is my shepherd.
He gives me everything I need.
He lets me rest in fields of green grass.
He takes me to pools of clear water.
He helps me on my way.
He protects me from danger.

From Psalm 23 of the Bible

Christians believe that God takes care of them in just the same way.

God is the good shepherd.

11 Let's look at
Being rescued

Imagine getting into danger.
How glad you are
when someone comes to help
and takes you to safety
without telling you off.

Christians believe that God loves
the people of this world.
The Bible is full of stories
of how God took care of his
people, the Israelites.
He rescued them when they were
slaves to the people in Egypt.

He brought them to a new land.
He helped them in battles against cruel enemies.
Even when they disobeyed him and were beaten,
he was always ready to forgive them and help them
again. This is what they said about God:

*Our God
is a God who saves,
he rescues us from death.*
From Psalm 68 of the Bible

God is a rescuer.

12 Let's look at
Friends

Hooray for friends.
Real friends.
People who like you
just as you are.
You can talk about anything together.
You can have fun or be quiet together.
You know your friend cares about you,
and will keep a promise.

Christians believe that God made people to be his friends. He cannot be friendly to those who do wrong but he is always ready to forgive anyone who is sorry. Here is a prayer from the Bible for people who want to be friends with God.

Dear God,
You have promised to forgive all the wrong things I have done.
I know you will teach me how to do right things
if I am willing to obey you ...
Dear God, you are the friend of those who obey you,
and you keep your promises.
From Psalm 25 of the Bible

God is a friend.

13 Let's look at

Air

Does air exist?
Of course it does!
Even though you cannot see air
you know it is there.
You feel the air that you breathe
to stay alive.
You feel the air moving,
blowing your hair;
hear it rustling the leaves,
see it bending the trees,
making the ocean waves...

The Bible says
that God is spirit.
Invisible as the wind,
but more powerful than a storm.
Unseen as the air we breathe,
but giving people new life.

God, who is spirit,
changes us.
His spirit fills us with
power, love and self-control.

**From Paul's second letter to the Christians in
Corinth and his second letter to Timothy, in the
Bible**

**God's unseen power
can change people ... and
the world.**

Who is God?

1   God is the maker of the world.

2   God is the giver of life.

3   God provides everything people need.

4   God is good.

5   God is always fair.

6   God has given laws to guide people.

7   God is a loving father.

8   God is like a loving mother.

9   God is like someone in your family who really understands and cares.

10 God is the good shepherd.

11 God is a rescuer.

12 God is a friend.

13 God's unseen power can change people ... and the world.

Book Two

The
Bible

A First Look
The Christian Faith

Bible passages mentioned in this book:

1   Genesis, chapter 1 to chapter 2, verse 4.

2   Genesis, chapter 6, verse 9 to the end of chapter 9; also Genesis, chapter 17, verses 1 to 8; also Luke, chapter 1, verses 67 to 79.

3   Psalm 78.

4   Exodus, chapter 20, verses 1 to 17.

5   Isaiah, chapter 40, verses 1 to 11.

6   Proverbs, chapter 15, verse 1, and chapter 11, verse 25; also, Ecclesiastes, chapter 7, verse 5.

7   Psalms 148 and 42.

8   Psalm 16.

9   Matthew, chapter 28.

10 Acts, chapter 12 and chapter 27.

11 Colossians, chapter 3, verse 12.

12 Psalm 119, verse 105.

13 2 Timothy, chapter 3, verse 15.

Contents

What is the Bible?   Introduction

Questions   1

Promises   2

Family stories   3

Rules   4

Reminders   5

Advice   6

Songs   7

Prayers   8

Life stories   9

Adventures   10

Letters   11

Light in the dark   12

Answers   13

Introduction
What is the
Bible?

The Bible is a book that is special to Christians. It is a collection of many different books—rather like a bookshelf with lots of different books in a row.

The books in the Bible were written by many different people at different times between 2,000 and 3,000 years ago.

The oldest books tell of the promises God made to a man called Abraham, and about how God looked after Abraham's descendants—the nation called Israel. These old books have always been special to the people of Israel. Today they are still the holy books of their descendants, the Jews.

Christians call these books the Old Testament.

The rest of the books in the Bible were written by the first people who believed in Jesus Christ—the first Christians.

Christians call these books the New Testament.

The Old Testament was written in Hebrew and the New Testament in Greek. Today, the books have been translated into the language you speak. Other people, in countries all over the world, have a Bible translated into their language too.

What is special about the Bible is that the writers all knew God—they loved and obeyed him.

● They wrote about the things God had told them.

● They wrote about the things God had done, so that other people would know what he was like and how he wanted them to live.

This book explores some of the most important things you will find in the Bible itself.

1 Let's look at

Questions

Why?
It's at the start of so many questions.
Why is the sky blue?
Why do birds sing?
Why do bees sting?
Why are people sometimes kind
and sometimes cruel?
Why were you born?

Genesis, the first book in the Bible,
begins with a story
about why the world is.
It says that God made the world
when there was nothing there:
he made earth and sky,
sun, moon and stars,
land and sea.
He made living things:
trees and flowers of all kinds,
fish, birds, and animals.
And he made people
to live in his world and to take care of it.

*God looked at everything he had made,
and he was very pleased.*

**From the first chapter of
Genesis, the first book in the
Bible**

**The Bible explains why the
world exists: because God
made it just as he wanted.**

2 Let's look at
Promises

If you make a promise you must keep it.

God has made promises.

Long ago, God sent a flood to get rid of all the badness in the world. Afterwards, God promised never to flood the world again. The rainbow is the sign of his promise.

Years later, God chose the nation called Israel to be his special people. God promised to take care of them.

There was one more promise. From the beginning, people had chosen to do bad things. It meant they could not be friends with God. The wrong they do makes them unhappy.

God promised to send someone to put things right.

Let us praise the Lord,
the God of Israel.
He has come to the help of his people
and has set them free.
He has sent someone to rescue them ...
as he promised long ago.

From the book Luke wrote, in the New Testament

Christians believe that God kept that promise by sending his own son, Jesus, to show people how they could be friends with God again.

The Bible tells people about God's promises to care for them and for the world.

3 Let's look at

Family stories

Can you remember when
you were really little?
All those memories
are the first part
of the story of your life.
It is just a little part
of the story of your family.

The Bible tells the story
of a family that became a whole
nation: the people of Israel.
It's a true story
and it began nearly 4,000 years ago.
God gave them a land to live in
and told them what they must do
to be happy.
And whatever they did—in good times and bad—
he still loved them.

We will tell our children
and our grandchildren
about God's power
and the great and wonderful
things he has done.

From Psalm 78, in the Old Testament

**The Bible tells the story of God
and his people, and shows how
much God loves everyone.**

4 Let's look at
Rules

When you have rules
you know what you can do
and what you can't do.
Good rules
are there to help you,
and they make you
feel safe.

44

The Bible says that
God gave his people rules
which told them how they
should live
in order to be happy.
There were ten great rules—
the Ten Commandments.

I am your God: you must worship only me.
Do not worship anything or anyone else.
Never use my name as a swear-word.
Keep one special day of the week for resting.
Show respect for your father and mother.
Do not kill.
Husbands and wives,
keep your special love
for each other only.
Do not steal.
Do not tell lies.
Do not be jealous of what other people have.

From chapter 20 of the book called Exodus, in the Old Testament

The Bible gives God's rules for living a really happy life.

5 Let's look at
Reminders

So you forgot
what you were supposed to do.
Why didn't someone remind you
how important it was
to do as you were told?

The people of Israel kept forgetting
that God had chosen them.
They forgot his rules.
God sent special people—
the prophets—to warn them,
to remind them that disobeying God
would only lead to unhappiness.
The warnings were true:
the people lost battles
and were captured by their enemies.
God sent many prophets
to remind the people
that he still loved them,
still cared.

God says this:
*'Encourage my people;
tell them the good news
that I am coming to take
care of them
as a shepherd takes care
of little lambs.'*

**From the book written by a prophet called
Isaiah, in the Old Testament**

**The Bible tells people
how important it is to
remember God.**

6 Let's look at
Advice

Good advice is really helpful.
When you don't know what to do,
when you feel muddled or worried,
it's nice to have someone
to make things clear.

The Bible has whole books
of good advice
for people who want to live in
the best way.
They talk about everything—
big and little—
that happens in life.

*A gentle answer
can stop someone
being angry.*

**From a book of wise sayings
called Proverbs, in the Old
Testament**

If you help others
you will be helped.

Another of the Proverbs

It's better to have wise people tell you off
than to have silly people
say how great you are.

From a book of wisdom, called Ecclesiastes,
in the Old Testament

The Bible has wise sayings to help people
live in the right way day by day.

7 Let's look at
Songs

Sometimes, when you are happy,
you want to sing and dance for joy.
Sometimes, when you're miserable,
a sad song seems to understand.

In the Bible are songs written long ago
by people who loved God.
There are happy songs,
and sad songs.

*Let everything
in all the world
sing praise to God:
the sun, the moon,
the stars, the skies,
the land, the sea,
the plants, the animals,
and all the people:
for God made them all.
God is great.*

**From the songbook of the Bible, the
book called Psalms**

As a deer longs for a drink of cool water
so I long for you, dear God . . .
I am so sad, so unhappy
and I don't know why—
but I will look to God to help me,
God the rescuer,
and then I will be able to sing
happy songs again.

Another of the Psalms

For hundreds of years, the people who love God
have used these songs to tell God what they're
thinking and how they're feeling.

**The Bible has songs to sing to God—songs for
happy times, sad times, and all times!**

8 Let's look at
Prayers

It's good to have a friend
you can really talk to—
someone who will listen
to whatever you have to say;
someone who will be glad to hear
your good news;
someone who will stay close
when you're lonely;
someone who is strong when you
need help.

The people who love God
talk to him as a friend:
they say prayers.
In the Bible there are prayers
by people who lived long ago,
who loved God
and spent time talking to him.

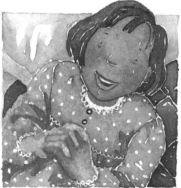

Dear God,
You give me all I need.
You guide me in what I should do.
You always keep me safe.
How happy I am to spend time
with you.
From the book of Psalms

**The Bible has prayers that help
people learn how to talk to God.**

9 Let's look at
Life stories

What makes people famous?
Why do crowds rush to see them?
What is their life story?
Who will tell you about them?

In the New Testament part of the Bible
there are four stories about a famous person:
Jesus Christ.
Each story is a bit different,
because it was written by a different person:
Matthew, Mark, Luke and John.
They wrote down the things Jesus said about God,
and about how people should live.
They told the stories of how he healed people.
They remembered the day he was put to death
and the day he came to life again.
They remembered the day he went back to heaven.
They wanted to spread the good news
that Jesus was God's Son,
who came to live in the world
to make people God's friends again.

Before he went back to heaven
Jesus said to the group of his special friends,
'Go to all people everywhere.
Tell them about me
so they can follow me
and live as God wants them to.'

From the very end of the book Matthew wrote about Jesus

The Bible tells people about Jesus, so that they can believe in him too.

10 Let's look at

Adventures

It's exciting to read about great adventures
of people setting off to do great deeds.

The book of Acts in the Bible
tells the story of the followers of Jesus,
and their adventures.
God gave them the courage
to spread Jesus' message of new life
to many different countries.

They faced many dangers:
they were put in prison,
shipwrecked,
left with very little money…
but they were so sure that
God was helping them
that they carried on with
their great task with joy.
Their message—
the Christian faith—
changed the world.

**The Bible tells the story of
the first Christians and
shows how God helped
them spread the news
about Jesus.**

11 Let's look at

Letters

Why write a letter?
There are thank-you-very-
much letters,
missing-you letters,
wish-you-were-here letters,
get-well-soon letters,
I've-got-great-news letters.
Isn't it wonderful to get a letter
from a friend?

The followers of Jesus
wrote letters to the new groups of Christians:
thanking them for their help;
saying how much they missed them;
asking for prayers for people who were unwell;
and telling them more about Jesus
and how they should live.

You are the people of God:
he loved you
and chose you for his own.
So you must be kind
to one another . . .
be patient,
and forgive each other
just as God has forgiven you.

From a letter written by a Christian leader
named Paul to the Christians in the ancient
town of Colossae

The Bible has letters written to new Christians that
explain how Jesus wants them to live.

12 Let's look at

Light in the dark

Imagine being in the dark,
not knowing where to go,
what to do;
bumping into things by mistake,
getting hurt,
getting into danger.

The Bible says
that what God has told people
in its pages
about himself
and about how to live
is like a light in the dark:
it helps people see their way safely
through life.

Dear God,
What you say is a lamp to
guide me
and a light for my path.

From Psalm 119

**The things that God tells
people in the Bible can
help guide them when life
is difficult, like a light in
the dark.**

13 Let's look at
Answers

When you have a problem
you feel stuck.
But when you have an answer
you know what to do.

Many people
who wonder what life is for
and how they should live it
find answers in the Bible.
There they read
that God made them,
that God loves them,
and that God sent Jesus
to make them his friends,
so they could be happy
for ever.

*Since you were a child
you have studied the scriptures.
They have made you truly wise
so that you understand
how Jesus can help you
if you believe in him.*

From the letter that a Christian leader named Paul wrote to a young Christian named Timothy. The Bible is sometimes called 'scripture'.

The Bible teaches people how Jesus can help them to be really happy.

What is the Bible?

1   The Bible explains why the world exists: because God made it just as he wanted.

2   The Bible tells people about God's promises to care for them and for the world.

3   The Bible tells the story of God and his people, and shows how much God loves everyone.

4   The Bible gives God's rules for living a really happy life.

5   The Bible tells people how important it is to remember God.

6   The Bible has wise sayings to help people live in the right way day by day.

7   The Bible has songs to sing to God—songs for happy times, sad times, and all times!

8   The Bible has prayers that help people learn how to talk to God.

9   The Bible tells people about Jesus, so that they can believe in him too.

10 The Bible tells the story of the first Christians and shows how God helped them spread the news about Jesus.

11 The Bible has letters written to new Christians that explain how Jesus wants them to live.

12 The things that God tells people in the Bible can help guide them when life is difficult, like a light in the dark.

13 The Bible teaches people how Jesus can help them to be really happy.

Book Three
Jesus

A First Look
The Christian Faith

Bible passages mentioned in this book:

1   Luke, chapter 1, verses 67 to 79.
2   Matthew, chapters 5 to 7.
3   John, chapter 6, verses 1 to 14 and 25 to 59.
4   John, chapter 4, verses 1 to 41.
5   John, chapter 15, verses 1 to 17.
6   John, chapter 14, verses 1 to 7.
7   John, chapter 10, verses 1 to 10.
8   John, chapter 10, verses 11 to 16.
9   John, chapter 8, verse 12 and chapter 9, verses 1 to 7.
10 John, chapter 11, verses 1 to 25.
11 Luke 23, especially verse 34.
12 Luke 24, especially verses 4 to 5.
13 John, chapter 14, verses 16 to 17 and chapter 16, verse 7.

Contents

Who is Jesus?   Introduction

Dark times   1

Happiness   2

Being hungry   3

Being thirsty   4

Trees in blossom   5

Finding your way   6

Gates   7

People who protect us   8

Light   9

Being alive   10

A new start   11

Incredible news   12

Special friends   13

Introduction
Who is
Jesus?

One of the first things
that people learn about Jesus
is that he is
the Christmas baby.

Some people believe
that Jesus was a very special person:
God's Son.

Jesus lived about 2,000 years ago.
But ever since, people have heard about
what he said and did
and have wanted to follow him—
to be Christians.

Now there are many, many Christians
all around the world.
Christians believe that Jesus came to show
people how they could be friends with God.

The New Testament part of the
Bible includes stories of his life
written by four different people:
Matthew, Mark, Luke and John.

In this book you will discover some
of the things they tell us:

- about Jesus' birth

- about the things he did and
  the things he said

- about his death—and his
  coming alive again

- about his promise of a new
  kind of life for anyone who
  believes in him

1 Let's look at

Dark times

Do you ever wake up early when the world outside is dark and scary? You wait eagerly for the very first sign of light to show that day is coming.

Sometimes, when things do not go right, you may think that daytime feels as gloomy as night.

That is how the people called the Jews felt two thousand years ago in Israel.
God seemed far away from them, and foreigners, the Romans, had conquered their land. But they believed that God would send someone to rescue them.

Just a little while before Jesus was born one of his relatives, Zechariah, said this:

*'God will send
the one who will rescue us...
it will be like the sunrise
after the darkness.'*

From the book Luke wrote about Jesus

God sent special messengers—angels—who said that this someone was Jesus: God's son. They said so to his mother Mary, to her husband, Joseph, and to shepherds on a hillside.

**Jesus' birth was like the first light of dawn.
People believed he would grow up to make their sad, dark world bright and joyful.**

2 Let's look at

Happiness

When you do something
that you know is right
you feel happy inside.

Jesus knew about happiness.
He grew up with his family.
He played with other children
when he was little.
When he grew older, he learned
the family trade and became a
carpenter.

Then, when he was a man,
he began a new kind of work.
With a few special friends,
his disciples, he travelled around
telling people about God.

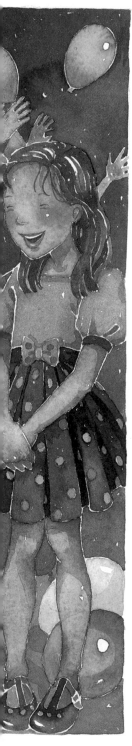

He told them how they could be really happy by living as God wants:
showing love and kindness to everyone,
even enemies;
not staying angry
but sorting out quarrels;
not trying to get revenge,
but doing good;
not worrying about how to get rich,
but helping those in need,
not pointing out other people's mistakes but being sorry for their own mistakes.

Jesus said:
'The people who live in the way that God wants are truly happy.'
From the book Matthew wrote about Jesus

Jesus taught people how to live as God wants, so that they will be truly happy.

3 Let's look at

Being hungry

Think how hungry you feel when a meal is late...
When it comes at last you eat and eat.
Then you're so full you can eat no more.
But in a while you're hungry again.

One day, thousands of people came
to listen to Jesus.
But they had not brought any food to eat.
A little boy had brought his lunch along:
five round, flat loaves and two small fish.
Jesus thanked God for this food,
and God made it into enough for everyone.
Jesus' disciples shared it out.

But Jesus said
that tummies full of food
aren't all that people need.

'There is another kind of food
that people need even more.
God wants you to believe in me—
because God has sent me
to give you life that will last
for ever.
Then you will never again feel
hollow, and empty, and lost.'

From the book John wrote about Jesus

Believing in Jesus is like having a meal—
and the good feeling lasts and lasts!

Jesus said:
'I am the bread of life.'

4 Let's look at
Being thirsty

Think of a hot summer day:
you have been playing for hours
and now you need
a long, cool drink.

In Israel, the country where Jesus lived,
it is hot and dry all summer long.
One day, Jesus stopped by a well.
He asked a woman who was there
to pull up a bucket of water
so that he could have a drink.

And then he said
that he could give her special water to drink
and she would never be thirsty again!
    The woman was very surprised
because Jesus hadn't got a bucket.
He explained
that when people long to be friends with God
it is like longing for a cool, refreshing drink.
Jesus said that he could help her
to be friends with God.

From the book John wrote about Jesus

Jesus said: 'I can give you life-giving water.'

5 Let's look at
Trees in blossom

Trees in blossom
look so lovely...
you want to cut off
bits of branch
and take them
home.

But the flowers soon die
when they are cut off a plant.
If you leave them growing
they will produce
seeds and fruit.

In the country where Jesus lived there were fields of vines which produce grapes. And he was thinking about how they grow when he said this to his friends:

'The people who believe in me are like branches on a vine. If you belong to me, just as branches belong to the trunk and the roots, then you will grow and flourish like a branch that produces lots of fruit. But if you break off from me then you will be like a useless branch that dries up and dies.'

From the book John wrote about Jesus

Jesus said: 'I am the real vine.'

79

6 Let's look at

Finding your way

Have you ever stepped off the
path you know
and gone off on your own?
It seems exciting to explore
somewhere new...
but what happens if you can't
find your way home?

In the beginning,
the Bible says,
God made people who
would know him
and be his friends.
But instead they wanted their
own way
and lived selfishly.

Jesus told his followers
that he was going to make
a new home for people
where they would be with
God again.

'But where is that place?'
asked a friend called Thomas,
'and how can we know the way there?'
   Jesus said:
'I am the only way
that will take people back to God
to be with him for ever.'

From the book John wrote about Jesus

Jesus said: 'I am the way.'

7 Let's look at
Gates

Think of running to your home...
Will the gate be unlocked
so that you can open it quickly
and go in to where you are
safe?

Jesus said that people long
to be with God,
to be safe with him
and to live as he wants.
But how can they get to God?

Jesus said:
'I am the gate
that will take you to God.
You will be safe with him,
as sheep are inside a
sheep-fold.'

From the book John wrote about Jesus

Jesus said: 'I am the gate.'

8 Let's look at
People who protect us

If someone is taking care of you
it's good to know
that they won't run off
if things get scary.

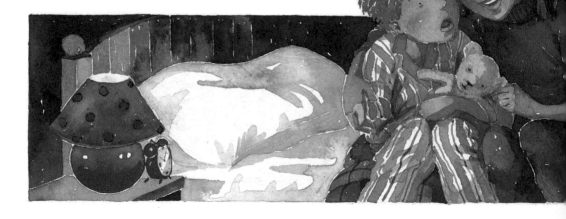

The shepherds in Israel
in the time of Jesus
had to protect their sheep
from all kinds of danger.
But if a wolf came by
and things looked dangerous
a bad shepherd might run off.

The good shepherd
would stay and protect his
sheep even if he had to risk
his life to save them.
Jesus said that he would
take care of people
just as a shepherd takes
care of sheep.

Jesus said:
'I am the good shepherd.
My sheep are the people
who follow me.
I know my sheep,
and my sheep know me.
I will look after them
really well.
I will even die for them.'

From the book John wrote about Jesus

**Jesus said: 'I am the
good shepherd.'**

9 Let's look at
Light

Light is great:
you can see what you're doing
and where you're going.

Sometimes people who were blind came to Jesus
and he gave them back their sight:
wonderful daylight
instead of a world of darkness.

But Jesus said
it wasn't only blind people
who were in the dark.
Often, people can see well with their eyes
but they don't really understand
what they're doing
or what's going on around them.
It's like living in the dark.
What people really need to see
is what God wants them to do.

Jesus said
that the things he said and did
were like a light
that would show them.

Jesus said:
'I am the light of the world.
Whoever follows me
will have the light of life
and will never walk in
darkness.'
From the book John wrote about Jesus

Jesus said: 'I am the light of the world.'

10 Let's look at

Being alive

It's so sad when living things die
and you know they are gone
for ever.

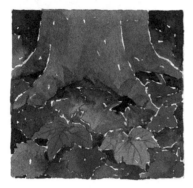

One day, people came to Jesus
and told him that his friend, Lazarus,
was very ill.
Would he please come
and heal him—
just as he had healed many others?
But when Jesus reached the place,
Lazarus had already died and was
buried in a stone grave.
His family and friends were crying...
And then Jesus brought Lazarus
back to life.

Jesus said:
'I am the one who gives life
even though there is death.
Whoever believes in me will live
even though their body dies.'

From the book John wrote about Jesus

God gave Jesus the power
to do a very special thing
that day to show people
that death is not the end,
because God is stronger
than death.

Jesus said: 'I am the resurrection and the life.'

11 Let's look at
A new start

When you've made a real mess
how can you begin to put it right?
If only someone loved you enough to do that for
you, so that you could make a fresh start.

The Bible says that people have made a mess of this
world because they do selfish things.
Jesus came to show them a better way
and to put things right.
He showed love and kindness to people
so that they could see how to live as God wants.
But this made some people angry:
they didn't like him telling them what God wanted.

Then one of Jesus' friends, Judas Iscariot,
let him down.
He told the people who were angry with Jesus
where they could find him alone.
They came and took him away to Pontius Pilate,
the Roman governor of their country.
They told lies about him
to get him into trouble.

So Jesus was put to death like
a criminal:
nailed to a cross of wood—
crucified.
Jesus did not argue.
He was loving and forgiving
even as he suffered.

*Jesus said: 'Father, forgive
them, for they do not know
what they are doing.'*
From the book Luke wrote about Jesus

**When Jesus died on a cross,
he showed people that God
loves them and forgives them,
and offers them a new start.**

12 Let's look at
Incredible news

Sometimes you hear news
that just doesn't seem possible.
You'd never believe it
unless you'd seen what happened.

The Roman soldiers put Jesus to death.
Then Jesus' friends took his body
and hurriedly buried it in a grave.
A day passed.
Then early the next morning
some of his followers went to the grave.
To their amazement
the huge stone that had blocked the entrance
had been moved aside.
They went inside the grave...
and the body of Jesus had gone.

*Two people in bright
shining clothes were there.
They said: 'Why are you
looking in a tomb
for someone who is alive?'*
From the book Luke wrote about Jesus

Later the same day,
and many times
for forty days afterwards,
Jesus' friends saw him.
They talked with him,
and shared meals with him.
They saw the marks of the nails
in his hands and feet.
God had brought him to life again—
death had been beaten.
Jesus' resurrection is the promise of
life with God for ever.

God brought Jesus back to life, and showed that he is indeed the life that death can never beat.

13 Let's look at
Special friends

Little children
often long for friends
who could help them feel brave and strong.

Imagine having a *real* friend
to help you in all you do.

Forty days after Jesus came back to life
he said goodbye to his friends,
and he went home to heaven.
His friends were there when it happened.
But Jesus made a promise to his friends:

Jesus said:
'I will ask God
to send you a special Helper,
who will stay with you all your life.
The Helper is called
the Holy Spirit,
who will show you what is right
and true.
It's better for you that I go
so that the Helper will come
instead.'

From the book John wrote about Jesus

The coming of this Helper meant that Jesus could be with them for ever, no matter where they went. Jesus also promised that one day he would come back and take his friends to be with him for ever.

Jesus went away from this world—but God sent his friends the Holy Spirit to help them live as God wants until he comes again.

Who is Jesus?

1   Jesus' birth was like the first light of dawn. People believed he would grow up to make their sad, dark world bright and joyful.

2   Jesus taught people how to live as God wants, so that they will be truly happy.

3   Jesus said: 'I am the bread of life.'

4   Jesus said: 'I can give you life-giving water.'

5   Jesus said: 'I am the real vine.'

6   Jesus said: 'I am the way.'

7   Jesus said: 'I am the gate.'

8   Jesus said: 'I am the good shepherd.'

9   Jesus said: 'I am the light of the world.'

10   Jesus said: 'I am the resurrection and the life.'

11   When Jesus died on a cross, he showed them that God loves them and forgives them, and offers them a new start.

12   God brought Jesus back to life, and showed that he is indeed the life that death can never beat.

13   Jesus went away from this world—but God sent his friends the Holy Spirit to help them live as God wants until he comes again.

Book Four
The
Church

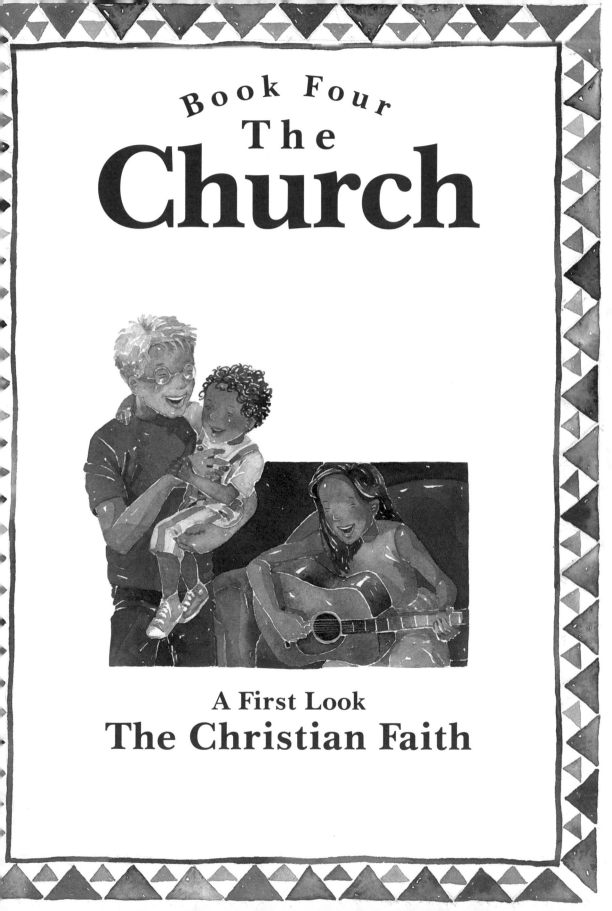

A First Look
The Christian Faith

Bible passages mentioned in this book:

1   Romans, chapter 8, verses 5 to 15

2   1 Peter, chapter 3, verse 21

3   Matthew, chapter 26, verses 26 to 30, Mark
    chapter 14, verses 22 to 26, Luke
    chapter 22, verses 14 to 20; See also 1
    Corinthians, chapter 11, verses 23 to 25

4   Hebrews, chapter 10, verse 25

5   Colossians, chapter 3, verse 16

6   1 John, chapter 1, verse 9

7   1 Peter, chapter 1, verse 3

8   Philippians, chapter 4, verse 6

9   Romans, chapter 12, verses 6 to 14

10 Colossians, chapter 3, verse 16

11 Matthew, chapter 28, verse 19

12 Philippians, chapter 2, verse 15

13 Romans, chapter 8, verses 38 to 39

Contents

What is the church? Introduction

Families   1

New beginnings   2

Remembering   3

Being together   4

Learning together   5

Saying sorry   6

Thank-yous   7

Asking   8

Living as a family   9

Celebrating!   10

Good news   11

Words or actions?   12

Grandparents   13

Introduction
What is the
Church?

Some people think that the church is a building. There *are* buildings called churches: special places where Christians meet to worship God.

They may have spires or towers, pillars and arches. They may have coloured windows, and the coloured glass may make a picture. Inside you might see carvings and candlesticks, and perhaps a cross...

Another church building might be quite plain, with bare white walls inside and rows of hard wooden seats...

Another might be a bright modern room with comfortable chairs arranged in a circle...

But if the building is empty, the real church isn't there...

The church is all the people who believe in Jesus Christ. They are called Christians.

There have been people called Christians for nearly 2,000 years, in many parts of the world. They meet in all kinds of church buildings and have different ways of worshipping God.

The special book of their faith, the Bible, explains how people first became Christians, how Christians should live, and what they should do together as a church.

In this book you will find out some of the things the Bible says about the church. It explains—

● what a Christian is

● why Christians meet together

● what they do at their meetings

● how their beliefs change the way they behave

● the message they want to tell other people

1 Let's look at
Families

Brothers and sisters
are different from friends.
They have been born into
or made into
a family.
They belong to each other.

Everyone is part of a human family.
The Bible says that people
can belong to another family:
God's family.

It's only human to do wrong things.
That cannot please God
because God is good.
But Jesus came
to help people change,
to put things right
between them and God.
When people believe that,
God makes them his children
and they can call God
Daddy.

From the letter Paul wrote to the
first Christians in Rome

Every Christian belongs
to God's family.
God is their father.
Other Christians are their
brothers and sisters.

The church is the family
of Christians.

2 Let's look at
New beginnings

Some days
everything goes wrong.
If only you could begin the day again.
If only you could be good.

Christians believe
that God helps people start again.

There is a special event
called baptism
when people are washed
with water
to show they are making
a new start
as God's children.

*Baptism is not the washing away
of ordinary dirt;
it is the sign of a new beginning
and a promise to live in a way
that pleases God.*

From the first letter Peter wrote to new Christians

**When people join God's family,
the church, they are making a
new beginning.**

3 Let's look at
Remembering

Does your family celebrate special events?
Do you have a meal together
and talk about what you are celebrating?
Do you say: 'Do you remember...?'

When they meet as a church,
the Christian family
shares a special meal.

This is how it began.

*It was the time of a Jewish celebration
called the Passover. Jesus was sharing a
meal with his friends. He took a loaf,
broke it into pieces and shared it out.*

*'Eat this now,' he said. 'And every time
you share bread together like this,
remember I have given my life for you.'*

*Then he took a cup of wine, and shared it
with them. 'Drink this,' he said. 'And when
you share wine like this, remember
I have given my life for you.'*

**From the books that Matthew, Mark
and Luke wrote about Jesus**

The very next day, Jesus was killed.
But God brought him to life again.
Christians believe that those who
follow Jesus start a new life too:
a new life as God's friends for ever.

**Christians share bread and wine as a
church, to remember Jesus — and that he
gave his life for them.**

4 Let's look at
Being together

It's great when everyone in a family gets together
to talk, to share news, to do things.
You can help each other,
learn from each other,
have fun being together.

The Bible says
that the family of Christians
must meet together too.
Christians cannot help each other
if they never meet.

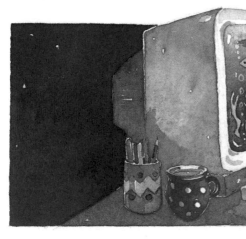

We, the family of God,
should be concerned about each other.
And we shouldn't forget to meet together—
as some do—
but get together to encourage each other.

From the letter written to a group of Hebrew Christians

Christians meet as a church to
help and encourage each other.

5 Let's look at

Learning together

It's fun to find things out for
yourself.
But it can be easier
to learn new things
from someone who really
knows.
And it's good to find out more
with people who are learning
just like you.

Christians want to find out more about God
and how he wants them to live:
how to show their love for him,
how to show their love for others.

When they meet as a church, they can learn together.
Those that are good at teaching
can help beginners understand more.
Christians can read the Bible together
and learn what it means.

Teach and instruct each other
as wisely as you can.

From the letter Paul wrote to the
first Christians in the city of Colossae

Christians learn about God — on their own and together as a church.

6 Let's look at
Saying sorry

When you do something wrong
you often wish you hadn't.
Then you want to say sorry
to those you have hurt.
You want them to forgive you,
so that the wrong thing can be
put right
and then forgotten.

If a group of people
have done wrong things
they may get together to say sorry
so that they can help each other
to do the right thing next time.

Christians are sad
when they do something wrong,
something that is not what God
wants. They know they must say
sorry to God as well as to the
person they have hurt.

*They want to tell him how sorry they are
that they have done wrong things.
They know that God will forgive them
and help them to do what is right.*

From the first letter John wrote to new Christians

**Christians say sorry to God for the wrong
things they have done — on their own
and together as a church.**

7 Let's look at
Thank-yous

When someone gives you a present,
or does something really kind,
you want to say thank you.
It shows the person
how happy you are
and it makes them happy too.

When Christians meet
they say thank you to God:
for the world he has made
and all the good things it provides;
for being a loving father to them,
for helping and guiding them
in all they do.

*Let us always give thanks to God
who has given us new life.*

From the first letter Peter wrote to new Christians

**Christians say thank you to God for
his goodness to them — on their
own and together as a church.**

8 Let's look at
Asking

Dare you ask
for the things you really want?
Or will you get into trouble
just for asking?

What Christians want
more than anything else
is to know God better.

They also want to ask God
to give them the things
they need.
They want God to keep
them safe, to help them to
live in the right way
and to help other people.

They want God to take care of the world.
They want God's help
to tell other people about Jesus.
They know that God wants
to do all these things for them.

*Don't worry
about anything,
but pray to God
and ask him
for everything
you need,
and thank him
for his goodness.*

**From the letter Paul wrote to the first
Christians in the city of Philippi**

**Christians ask God for
the things they need —
on their own and
together as a church.**

9 Let's look at
Living as a family

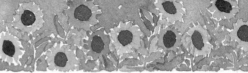

In a loving family
people work together
and really help each other.

The Bible tells Christians to help each other
like members of a family.
Because each person is different,
everyone has a special gift to share,
and each one of them is important.

*God has given
each Christian
a different job to do
in the church family.
For example,
some are able to teach others
more about God,
some are good at sharing
their things,
some know how to encourage
others,
some are good at welcoming
people into their homes.
God tells his family to
celebrate with people who
are happy
and to comfort those who are
sad.*

**From the letter Paul wrote to the
first Christians in Rome**

**The family of Christians care
for one another and for other
people in everyday ways.**

10 Let's look at
Celebrating!

The best way
to celebrate good news
is to have a party!

The good news
that Christians share
is that God has given them
a new beginning in life.
They know they are children of God
and that they are with God
for ever.

Everyone is welcome
to join God's family.
It is a life full of joy
which makes them want to sing.
Christians love to celebrate together.

Give thanks to God;
sing psalms, and hymns
and songs of praise.

From the letter Paul wrote to the
first Christians in the city of Colossae

There are special celebrations at times like Christmas, when Christians remember Jesus' birth. At Easter, they are sad because Jesus was killed, and then they celebrate because God gave him new life.

Christians celebrate together, and sing joyful songs. They have festivals to remember special events.

11 Let's look at
Good news

If you have good news
you want to tell everyone.
You don't sit in a corner
wondering if people will ask
what you're thinking about.
You just have to tell them
out loud.

Christians have good news to tell:
that Jesus loves everyone
and that anyone who believes in him
can be really happy
because God accepts them into his family
and gives them a new start.
Jesus said this to the friends who first believed in him:

*Go out to everyone
and tell them about me
so they can follow me.*

**From the book Matthew wrote
about Jesus**

**Christians want to tell
other people about
Jesus Christ.**

12 Let's look at

Words or actions?

It's one thing
to *say* you want to be good.
But it's when you show this
by doing good things
that people really believe you.

God wants everyone to be good
and to do good things:
God's family must be different
from those people who choose to
do wrong.
God wants them to be loving and
kind,
unselfish and fair,
to speak kindly,
to share what they have,
to help those in need.

In this way they can show people
a little of what God's love is like.
And they provide an example
of how God wants people to live.

Christians must live shining lives,
like stars lighting up the sky.

From the letter Paul wrote to the
first Christians in the city of Philippi

Christians want to please God by doing good
so everyone can see what he is like.

Grandparents

Your family
is not just you
and your parents,
but also your grandparents
and great-grandparents...
people from long ago, and far away.

The Christian family
includes everyone
who believes in Jesus:
from the first special friends he chose,
those who knew him as a man on this earth,
to people today who believe in him.

It includes all kinds of Christians
in countries all round the world
for 2,000 years.

Some are famous and remembered in
special stories,
others are not:
but they are all God's family
and God knows each one.
He has promised all of them
he will be with them for ever.

*Nothing—
not even death—
can separate us
from the love of God.*

**From the letter Paul wrote to
Christians in Rome**

**The church is the family of Christians
throughout the ages.**

What is the church?

1 The church is the family of Christians.

2 When people join God's family, the church, they are making a new beginning.

3 Christians share bread and wine as a church, to remember Jesus — and that he gave his life for them.

4 Christians meet as a church to help and encourage each other.

5 Christians learn about God — on their own and together as a church.

6 Christians say sorry to God for the wrong things they have done — on their own and together as a church.

7 Christians say thank you to God for his goodness to them — on their own and together as a church.

8 Christians ask God for the things they need — on their own and together as a church.

9 The family of Christians care for one another and for other people in everyday ways.

10 Christians celebrate together, and sing joyful songs. They have festivals to remember special events.

11 Christians want to tell other people about Jesus Christ.

12 Christians want to please God by doing good so everyone can see what he is like.

13 The church is the family of Christians throughout the ages.

A First Look: The Christian Faith contains

Book One: God 1–32

Book Two: The Bible 33–64

Book Three: Jesus 65–96

Book Four: The Church 97–128